C000302634

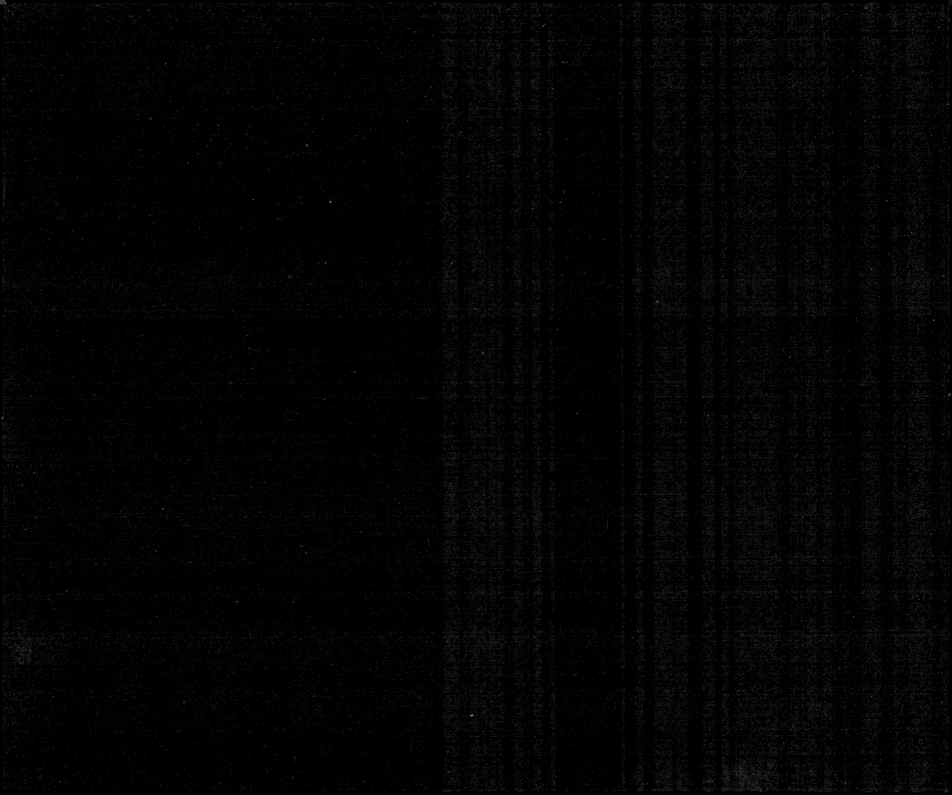

'SOUTHERN REGION MEMORIES'

PHOTOGRAPHS FROM THE BLUEBELL MUSEUM ARCHIVE

Compiled by John Sharp and Tony Hillman

ISBN 978-1-906419-48-6

First published in 2010 by Kevin Robertson under the **NOODLE BOOKS** imprint
PO Box 279, Corhampton, SOUTHAMPTON. SO32 3ZX

www.noodlebooks.co.uk

Printed in England by Ian Allan Printing Ltd.

Front cover - Pullman cars being worked south for attention at Preston Park Works were sometimes added (locked out) to the formation of a service train. One such regular working was the 2.45 pm Redhill to Brighton train, which John Smith photographed a number of times departing from Redhill behind 'D' class 4-4-0s. Class member No. 31737 heads south, passing the locomotive sheds, on Wednesday 13 April 1955. This engine is the one member of the class now preserved as part of the National collection. (5-124-1)

Frontispiece - The tranquil setting of a country branch line, represented here on what is unmistakably the route to Lyme Regis. No. 30584, which together with her two sisters, had long been pensioned off from its original use as a suburban tank and now finds use on the borders of Devon and Dorset. The service is the 11.05 a.m. to Axminster on Saturday 21 August 1954, recorded between Combpyne and the viaduct. Further west, three other former suburban tank engines of even older vintage, the Beattie 'Well Tanks' were similarly employed on the Wenford Bridge branch. (5-95-5)

Opposite page - 'Battle of Britain' class pacific No. 34055 'Fighter Pilot' seen north of Horam on Saturday 2 July 1960 with the 9.05 a.m. Polegate to Heathfield special freight, conveying fertilizer products. (3-35-1)

Rear cover - No. 34039 'Boscastle' holding up the traffic at Edinburgh Road level crossing on the Portsmouth North Dockyard branch with a test train of Pullman stock, Sunday, 20 November 1960. At the time consideration was being given to the use of the branch for Royal workings previously accommodated at the Harbour Station, the existing arrangement not being considered totally satisfactory - hence the test. Further views of the trials carried out at this time will be found later in this book. (3-57-2)

INTRODUCTION BY TONY HILLMAN

It was back in February 2007 that a friend phoned to tell me John J Smith had died. (Similar in name, but unrelated to the also deceased John Smith of Lens of Sutton). I was told John J Smith had amassed a large collection of both Southern Railway and Southern Region archive material and did I think the Bluebell Railway Museum would be interested? Without really knowing what might be involved I said that I was sure we would. Little could we have known that this would start a project that continues to this day. The actual volume of material is enormous, just the sorting and cataloguing will continue for many months, possibly years into the future.

Around the end of 2007 we opened one of the storage crates to find some shoeboxes full of negatives. All neatly stored in envelopes, and with date and location written on the outside. In total there were nine shoeboxes, containing over 6000 negatives. I don't think any of us realized the significance of these negatives at the time, but we decided to get some professionally scanned and printed. When the results came through it was clear that the photographs were excellent. The pictures were nearly all trains or locomotives, but it was obvious even from this small sampling that we had something rather special. The decision was thus taken to have all the negatives similarly dealt with, a process which took nearly a year.

To make the views available to enthusiasts, a section of the Bluebell Museum website was created where the pictures were displayed and indexed. As collectors found the site, we became aware that many people knew of John Smith's work and were able to fill us in on his background. From discussion it quickly became clear that the pictures were not just well composed but the content of many was special too. The collection includes numerous unusual workings or motive power.

John Smith worked for British Railways at Croydon in the Divisional Office. In his collection were many certificates showing he had taken signalling exams but he seems to have worked for much of his time in the Special Trains area. This, of course, is the reason that he knew about the interesting workings he photographed. In discussion with one of his ex-colleagues I was told that on at least one occasion the unusual motive power was actually specified by John himself!

This book may appear at first sight to just contain superb pictures of the Southern Region era. But read the captions and you will find that many pictures are unusual in some way or other. We also believe that many of the pictures have never been published before.

I should like to thank John Sharp for agreeing to collect together the pictures for this book and creating the captions. His knowledge of Southern Region workings is second to none. Also, without the continued assistance of Roger Merry-Price, Martin Elms and Roger Cruse, the whole John Smith project would probably not have got off the ground. Finally, a big thank you to Chris Turner who was the first to contact me about the collection. Without his intervention the whole lot could have ended up in a skip. The captions have been checked using the 'Railway Observer' and we thank the RCTS for producing this fine reference collection.

We all hope that in the not to distant future the Bluebell Railway Museum will have an archive facility where access to all the archive material the Bluebell owns can be made available to the public. All the proceeds from this book are being donated to that cause.

The John J Smith photographic collection is available on the Bluebell Museum website www.bluebell-railway-museum.co.uk Click on **The Archive** followed by **Photographic Archive.** The photograph reference number is included in each caption.

We both start and end this book with views of special workings to and from the same venue. The various sports events at Wembley Stadium provided the interesting spectacle of excursions from all regions to Wembley Stadium and Wembley Central stations, those from the Southern Region being worked throughout by Southern motive power. Seen at Neasden on Saturday 11 March 1961 after being relieved of the empty stock and turning on the stadium loop, are Nos. 34016 'Bodmin' and 34089 '602 Squadron', which will now head to Neasden depot for servicing. (Notice the Metropolitan line electric locomotive on its train in the background.) No. 34016 had arrived with the 9.55 am unadvertised excursion (W947) from Poole, and No. 34089 the 10.46 am from Canterbury East. Both trains were in connection with the Women's International Hockey Final. (3-65-5)

Above - Having been repaired, or as appears from the fresh paint, overhauled at Preston Park, Pullman Brake Car No. 80 had earlier found its way to East Croydon on the first stage of its journey back to the Eastern Region. 'C2X' 0-6-0 No. 32547 has charge of the vehicle as the 3.00pm East Croydon - Canonbury working seen passing Kentish Town West on Saturday 24 September 1955. (1-22-4)

Right - Having arrived at Canonbury, the 'C2X' was detached and Eastern Region 'N2/2' class 0-6-2T No. 69547 coupled to the opposite end of the car for the conclusion of its journey to Finsbury Park. (1-22-5)

Above - Brighton based 'West Country' class pacific No. 34045 'Ottery St.Mary' has recently taken over haulage of the 11.5 a.m. Walsall-Hastings train and is passing Chelsea & Fulham on Saturday, 24 August 1957. This engine would be rebuilt in October 1958 and transferred to Nine Elms Depot. (6-36-6)

Right - Wrong line working always provided something different for the photographer. Here 'Schools' class 4-4-0 No. 30905 'Tonbridge' steams into the cramped confines of St.Leonards Warrior Square station, with a Hastings - Charing Cross train on Saturday, 23 February 1952. The engineers were occupying the 'up' line. (4-38-7)

Left - 'Take 1' (perhaps!). 'M7' class 0-4-4T No. 30026, disguised not very convincingly as No. 26 at Baynards Station taking a leading role during filming for BBC TV's Childrens Hour series 'The Railway Children'. Sunday, 17 February 1957. (6-2-1)

Above - "All aboard!". It would seem that nobody wants to be left behind during this filming sequence for Horizon Films at Fittleworth. Double-domed 'C2X' class 0-6-0 No. 32535 takes part with three (and a bit) Western Region carriages on Sunday, 15 November 1959. (7-93-6)

Left - Milk trains were a daily sight around the Capital, the more insignificant among them usually escaping the camera lens. Here, 'O1' class 0-6-0 No. 31048 trundles by Chelsea & Fulham Signalbox on Saturday, 24 August 1957, with the 3.26 p.m. train from East Croydon to Wood Lane. (6-37-1)

Above - With an age difference between them of nearly 60 years, 'C' class 0-6-0 No. 31719 trundles by Harringay Park Junction hauling brand new electric locomotive No. E5002, which is en-route from Doncaster Works to Stewarts Lane Depot, Wednesday, 13 May 1959. (7-32-8)

Above - '4-RES' unit No. 3072, minus its dining car but including Pullman car 'Brenda', departing Redhill as empty stock bound for Lovers Walk Depot, Brighton, on Friday, 2 November 1956. 'Brenda' was usually to be seen in '6-PUL' unit No. 3013 so this is a curious working. The date is also long before '4-RES' operation ceased and the remaining units reformed as '4-PUL'. (1-94-4)

Opposite top - Tyneside parcels car No. E68000 arrived on the Central Section towards the end of 1955 for trials on parcels, empty stock and goods train workings. The vehicle provides an extraordinary sight on Monday, 5 December 1955, passing Earlswood with the 12.45 p.m Norwood Junction - Horsham freight. (1-26-1)

Opposite bottom - Track testing trials were conducted between Three Bridges and Haywards Heath on Sunday, 17 July 1960, using electric locomotives Nos. E5004 and 20001 plus diesel No. D6506 coupled together. In each direction, the leading engine hauled the other two. Here, E5004 leads the ensemble northbound through Balcombe. (3-40-8)

Opposite page - Ramblers excursions were a regular sight on Sundays, stations on the 'Bluebell' and 'Cuckoo' lines being popular destinations. 'Battle of Britain' class pacific No. 34068 'Kenley' is south of Kingscote with the 9.50 a.m. Victoria - Ardingly excursion on Sunday, 27 September 1959. (7-84-2)

Above - The roof-tops of North London at Camden Road and 'Schools' class 4-4-0 No. 30938 'St.Olave's' make for an unusual combination. The unidentified train is heading to its home region on Friday, 17 July 1959. (7-53-8)

Above - Engineers trains of varying descriptions provided additional interest on Sundays. 'E2' class 0-6-0T No. 32106 scurries along near Fishbourne Crossing on 10 January 1960 with track-laying vehicles en-route from Eastleigh to Three Bridges. (7-101-4)

Opposite top - 'N15' class 4-6-0 No.30740 'Merlin', withdrawn from service in December 1955, was used in a TV 'train crash' sequence, filmed on the Longmoor Military Railway in February 1956. The loco suffered comparatively little damage and was stored at Fratton Shed until being finally towed to Brighton Works for scrapping on Monday 7 May 1956. 'West Country' class pacific No. 34044 'Woolacombe' has been given this sombre duty and is seen pausing at Worthing Central with its charge. (1-48-3)

Opposite bottom - In this view, 'C' class 0-6-0 No. 31297 is emerging from the gloom at Holborn (Low Level) and is entering a bomb damaged area north of Holborn Viaduct Station with an engineers train on Sunday, 9 September 1956. (1-85-8)

Top - Weed-killing trains were a fascinating, if irregular, sight on country routes. Formed of an assortment of connected redundant tenders, 'Q' class 0-6-0 No. 30534 is seen near Hampden Park with one such train on Wednesday, 25 October 1950. (2-62-1)

Left - A rear view of a similar train in operation at the same location, Hampden Park, this time with 'Q' class No. 30546 propelling on a very wet Friday, 4 May 1951 (2-82-6)

Opposite - 'C' class 0-6-0 No. 31583 and 'K' class 2-6-0 No. 32346 are in charge of a weed-killing train on the 'Cuckoo Line', near Hellingly, Sunday, 3 June 1956, the formation this time consisting of tank wagons. (1-53-3)

Above - On Saturday, 21 December 1957, 'N' class 2-6-0 No. 31812 passes Pouparts Junction, Battersea, with an empty stock working conveying a Pullman car from St. Leonards to Eardley Carriage Sidings, Streatham. (6-52-1)

Right - 'E4' class 0-6-2T No. 32518 cautiously observes the speed restriction near Eastbourne Gas Works, on the single line known as 'The Crumbles siding', with a ballast train comprised of 7-plank wagons. Saturday, 28 October 1950. It was this location that had been used by the LBSCR for several of their official locomotive portraits recorded in 'photographic grey'. (2-62-2)

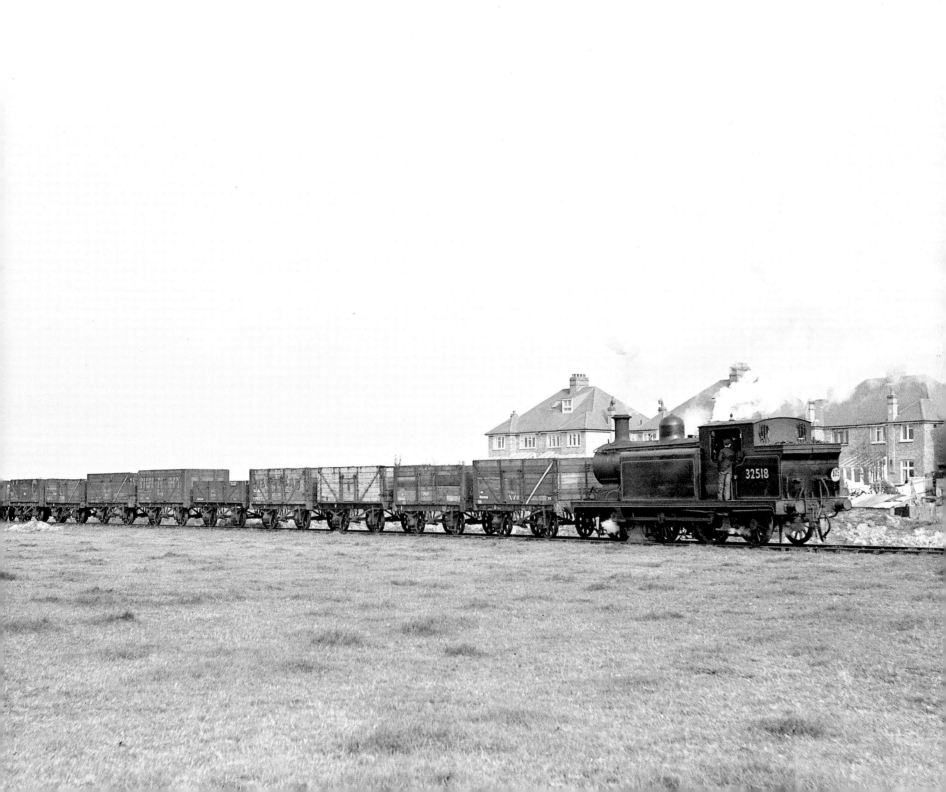

Considering the possibility of running Royal Trains to and from Portsmouth Dockyard, the Southern Region performed a series of tests on Sunday, 20 November 1960 over the North Dockyard branch from Portsmouth and Southsea (High Level) Station. Pacifics, Nos. 34075 '264 Squadron' and rebuilt sister, No. 34039 'Boscastle' worked the test train which was formed of Pullman cars 'Niobe' and 'Cassandra', Royal Saloon No. 396 and two B.R. Mk.1 coaches. The photographs show **Above -** 'Boscastle' about to take the branch from the High Level Station (3-56-6). **Opposite top -** No. 34075 '264 Squadron' crossing Edinburgh Road level crossing (3-57-4), and **Opposite bottom -** No. 34039 'Boscastle' trailing over Alfred Road level crossing (3-57-1). The worked distant signal, No. 15 at Portsmouth High Level, was 360 yards from the signal box and only 152 yards from its associated stop signal.

Above - On what was clearly a miserable wet day for the tests, No. 34075 is seen on the pier spur at Portsmouth & Southsea High Level station. (3-56-7)

Opposite - No. 34102 'Lapford' on the 'Portsmouth Direct' route with the diverted 10.26 am Bournemouth West - Waterloo service, Sunday 28 October 1962. The train was on this route due to blanketing of the formation on the down line between Swaythling and St Denys, although for the purpose, both the up and down lines were out of use. The train had made a special stop at Havant and another would come shortly at Guildford. (8-56-2)

On Thursday, 9 August 1956, two pacific hauled special trains to Margate via Canterbury East required assistance at Kearsney for the climb through Guston Tunnel and up Martin Mill Bank. The first of these (**above**) has the novel sight of tender-first 'O1' class 0-6-0 No. 31430 piloting 'Battle of Britain' class No. 34090 'Sir Eustace Missenden Southern Railway.' (1-79-1)

Right - The second special, with 'C' class 0-6-0 No.31243 assisting 'Battle of Britain' class No. 34083 '605 Squadron'. Both trains are seen on Kearsney loop. (1-79-2)

Above - 'M7' class 0-4-4-T No. 30053 makes a pleasant sight passing Falmer on Sunday 13 May 1956, with the 10.20 a.m. Brighton to Hastings vans, a theatrical company 'props' special working. (1-48-5)

Opposite top - Unlike the individual special seen earlier, ex-works Pullman cars being returned from Preston Park Works could also be seen in passenger trains, as witness recently to traffic Standard 4MT No. 80104, passing Holywell with the 5.18pm Brighton to Victoria train, which on this day also conveys pullmans 'Car.No.55', 'Chloria' and 'Car No.54', Friday, 22 April 1955. No. 80104 did not remain a Southern Region engine and by June 1955 was allocated to Plaistow. Holywell is now a favourite location for photographers on the Bluebell Railway and No. 80104 can currently be seen at Swanage. (5-125-3)

Opposite bottom - As a result of the severe flood damage caused to parts of the Kent Coast main line in January 1953, emergency workings were operated to serve Whitstable, Herne Bay and Birchington-on-Sea. By March, a motor train shuttle service was running between Faversham and Herne Bay using 'M7'class 0-4-4 tank engines transferred for the purpose from the Western Section. The 6.34 p.m. Herne Bay-Faversham train is near Chestfield & Swalecliffe Halt in the charge of No. 30053 on Sunday, 10 May 1953. (4-108-5)

Left - 'King Arthur' class 4-6-0 No. 30793 'Sir Ontzlake' is believed to be leaving Birchington-on-Sea with the 4.18 p.m. train to Ramsgate. Saturday, 2 May 1953. (4-103-1)

Bottom - Following the floods, the former spur between the ex.LCDR and ex.SER at Canterbury was reconnected for the use of trains from London to Ramsgate and Birchington-on-Sea. 'West Country' class pacific No. 34099 'Lynmouth' is approaching Canterbury West with the 3.35 p.m. Victoria to Birchington-on-Sea service on Saturday, 9 May 1953. (4-107-2)

Right - Also taken on the same day as the view of No. 34099 and with the spur seen on the left of the photograph, 'Battle of Britain' class pacific No. 34086 '219 Squadron' passes Canterbury 'B' Box with the 5.18 p.m. Margate to Ashford train. (4-107-6)

'Schools' class 4-4-0 No. 30917 'Ardingly' takes the Canterbury spur with the 2. 2 p.m. Birchington-on-Sea to Victoria train on Sunday, 10 May 1953. (4-108-1)

Engineers trains were a frequent sight on the main line via Faversham during the months following the floods. Veteran 'C' class 0-6-0 No. 31271 and 'Q1' class 0-6-0 No. 33022 double-head a track train near Chestfield & Swalecliffe Halt on Sunday, 10 May 1953. (4-108-4)

Above - Forest Hill Station on a miserable Saturday, 9 September 1950. 'D' class 4-4-0, No. 31488 is passing the long gone island platform with the 12.40 p.m. London Bridge - Maidstone West train. (2-50-1)

Left - A North London scene with 'E1' class 4-4-0 No. 31067 passing Queens Park with the 10.28 a.m. Sittingbourne - Camden vans on Thursday, 17 July 1958. It is probable the engine has travelled via the West London line and run around its train at Willesden Junction. (6-75-1)

'Battle of Britain' class pacific No. 34073 '249 Squadron' hurries through Horam on Sunday 18 August 1957, with the 7.9 p.m. Eastbourne to Romford return excursion comprised of Eastern Region stock. This train had been routed via the 'Cuckoo Line', Oxted and East Croydon, due to the lack of a suitable path on the main line via Haywards Heath. (6-36-1)

Basingstoke's 'T9' class 4-4-0 No. 30724 heads an Amesbury - Loughborough Junction troop train through Haydons Road on Saturday, 3 September 1955. Later in the day, the 'T9' worked the empty stock to Farnham. (1-19-1)

Opposite top - 'S15' class 4-6-0 No. 30499 is at Cricklewood on Saturday, 25 January 1958 with an unidentified special train working but noted by John Smith as having originated at Woking. (6-52-3)

Opposite bottom - As a consequence of engineering works in the Beckenham Junction area on Sunday 31 May 1959, main line services from Victoria (via Orpington) to the Kent Coast were diverted to run via Denmark Hill and Lewisham. Unkempt 'Battle of Britain' class pacific No. 34071 '601 Squadron' is approaching Lewisham with the 1.30 p.m boat train to Dover Marine. (7-39-1)

Bottom - Probably the real reason for John Smith's visit to Lewisham this Sunday was to photograph the down 'Golden Arrow', 2.00 p.m. Victoria to Folkestone Harbour, at an unusual location. 'Battle of Britain' class pacific No. 34085 '501 Squadron' is in charge, contrasting in external condition totally with '601 Squadron', also a 'Golden Arrow' engine in earlier years. (7-39-2)

'5-BEL' Pullman unit No.3051 is an unusual sight leaving Blackfriars as the 12.35pm service to Eastbourne on Wednesday, 19 April 1961 - note the extra passengers in the cab! It is possible that this train is chartered by a City company or newspaper group, such workings being noted in previous years. Car No. 88, the lead vehicle in the train, has recently been renovated by the 5BEL trust who are planning to restore a complete Brighton Belle set. (3-72-4)

Above - It would appear that a '5-BEL' 'Brighton Belle' Pullman unit has failed at Victoria on Sunday, 8 February 1959. 'Q' class 0-6-0 No. 30534 is in charge of the set seen passing Battersea Park en-route to Peckham Rye Electric Traction Depot. (7-3-4).

Opposite top - Electric locomotive No. E5008 and a filthy Standard class '5MT' 4-6-0 No. 73115 'King Pellinore' look a peculiar combination heading through Salfords with the heavy 5.14 p.m Newhaven Harbour - Victoria boat train on Thursday, 9 April 1964.(9-6-3)

Opposite bottom - Following a sojourn of eight months in Brighton Works, diesel locomotive No. 10800 heads a New Cross Gate to Brighton special test train through Salfords on Friday, 3 December 1954. The train is travelling on the down fast line on a 72 minute schedule. (5-112-4)

Above - An exhibition of British Railways locomotives and rolling stock was held at Eastbourne in June 1951 in connection with the International Union of Railways Conference. Black liveried electric locomotive No. 20003 heads a line of display locomotives featuring Standard classes '7MT' 4-6-2 No. 70009 'Alfred The Great', '4MT' 4-6-0 No. 75000 and '5MT' 4-6-0 No. 73001. Just visible is the Fell diesel No. 10100. Friday, 1 June 1951. (2-92-7)

Opposite top - Following the exhibition, No. 75000 departs from Eastbourne on Sunday, 3 June 1951, towing the diesel No. 10100 to London, Battersea, from which point, 10100 will be returned to the LMR and the Standard will run light engine to Swindon.(2-93-2)

Opposite bottom - A surprising visitor to Southern metals, the prototype 'Deltic', in company with diesel No. D8000, near Longhedge Junction on Friday, 21 June 1957, en-route from Willesden Junction to Battersea for display at the Modern Railway Exhibition, opened on 1 July 1957. (6-19-1)

Opposite top - 'U' class 2-6-0 No. 31627 is approaching Southfields with the 3.33 p.m. Clapham Junction (Windsor Lines) -Epsom horsebox special on Saturday, 15 September 1956. The centre conductor rail on this stretch of line serves London Transport's Earls Court - Wimbledon service. (1-86-1)

Opposite bottom - The 4.16 p.m. Mitre Bridge (ex.Newmarket) to Epsom horsebox special heads along the West London Line at Chelsea & Fulham behind 'U1' class 2-6-0 No.31898. Saturday, 8 August 1959. (7-63-1)

Above - A train of horseboxes, having travelled from the Eastern Region via Rotherhithe Tunnel, arrives at New Cross Gate behind 'J69/1' class 0-6-0T No. 68613, passing 'N' class 2-6-0 No. 31863 shunting empty stock in the down yard. Thursday, 31 August 1961. (8-8-6)

In sylvan surroundings, the 1.35 p.m. oil tank wagons for Norwood Junction are worked away from the Government Oil Store at Rowfant on Saturday, 28 June 1952, by 'E4' class 0-6-2T No. 32484 and 'Q' class 0-6-0 No. 30546. (4-69-4)

Forest Hill Bank, on the London Bridge to East Croydon line, provided a challenge to the crews of southbound goods trains. 'E2' class 0-6-0T No. 32104 has just cleared the platform at Brockley giving a helping hand to the 2.37 p.m. New Cross Gate - East Croydon freight on Saturday, 7 September 1957. The train engine is 'E4' class 0-6-2T No. 32473, now a Bluebell Railway locomotive. Travelling in the opposite direction is Bulleid 4SUB unit No.4702 displaying the headcode '90', indicating a London Bridge circular via Tulse Hill, Selhurst and Forest Hill. (6-38-6)

Left - 'D' class 4-4-0's are more usually noted on passenger trains but Brighton Shed has turned out No. 31734 for the Kemp Town branch goods on Saturday, 12 March 1955, seen passing Kemp Town Junction on its way back to Brighton at 12.25 p.m. The engine, based at Tonbridge Shed, had arrived at Brighton the previous day on the 2.45 pm Redhill - Brighton service train, attached to which was a Pullman kitchen car destined for Preston Park. (5-121-4)

Above - With Stewarts Lane Depot as a backdrop, 'C' class 0-6-0 No. 31267 approaches Longhedge Junction with the 12.3 p.m. Mottingham - Clapham Junction (West) milk empties, Saturday 10 March 1956. (1-30-3)

Left - 'K' class 2-6-0 No. 32342 heads down the Brighton main line at Salfords on Saturday, 22 August 1959 with the 7.40 a.m. Hoo Junction - Three Bridges oil train. Note the barrier safety wagons provided. (7-66-2)

Above - 'W' class 2-6-4 tank locomotives were not a common sight south of East Croydon but one was regularly used on the annual movement of vans accumulated throughout the year at Tattenham Corner. Class member No. 31920 pounds through Tadworth with the lengthy 10.28 a.m. Tattenham Corner - New Cross Gate working on Sunday, 14 December 1958. (6-103-4)

Stock movements for the new Clapham Museum

Top - Queens Road Battersea with 'M7' class 0-4-4T No. 30245 in charge of Midland Railway Dining car No. 3463 and 4-wheel North London Railway Directors Saloon No. 32 on Friday 25 September 1959. (7-82-5)

Left - Longhedge Junction, 'Schools' No. 30912 'Downside' hauling the new restored 'D' No. 737, but temporarily minus its chimney and en-route from Ashford Works. 22 June 1960. (9-95-14)

Opposite top - At Queens Road Battersea on 16 October 1959, is 'L' class 4-4-0 No. 31768 with Highland Railway vehicle No. 57A, The Duke of Sutherland's Saloon, built in 1899 and now at the NRM. (7-87-5)

Opposite bottom - The Midland Railway Third Dining Car built in 1914, and North London Director's Saloon seen earlier in their journey at Longhedge Junction on 18 September 1959, behind Stewarts Lane '4MT' 2-6-4T No. 42091.(7-82-3)

Above - A final view of the Clapham stock, again at Queens Road Battersea. 'Q1' No. 33013 recorded with the 1.53 SF GE - BO working, 2 October 1959 - the references 'GE' and 'BO' as appear in John Smith's notes concerning this working have not yet been explained. (7-85-1)

Opposite top - Standard class '4MT' 4-6-0 No. 75074 and 'N' class 2-6-0 No. 31410 storm through Clapham Junction with the 9.55 a.m. Victoria - Eardley Carriage Sidings 'Night Ferry' empty stock on Sunday, 31 January 1960. This was a day of disruption and diversion to services as the Eastern Section platforms at Victoria were closed for engineering works, continental traffic using Victoria (Central) throughout the day. (3-1-2)

Opposite bottom - 2MT class 2-6-2T No. 41292 is passing Wandsworth Road on Saturday, 6 June 1953, with a rake of empty pullman cars from Victoria which are bound for Eardley Carriage Sidings. (5-2-3)

Above - 'U1' class 2-6-0 No. 31899 and 'West Country' class pacific No. 34019 'Bideford' provide an unusual spectacle at Ashurst on Friday, 8 June 1962, working a Newcastle - Crowborough pigeon special consisting of seventeen Eastern Region bogie vehicles. (8-35-6)

Right - 'B4X' class 4-4-0 No. 2052 was one of several ex. LBSCR loco's loaned to the Western Section in connection with the Farnborough Air Show special traffic in July 1950. This particular locomotive was ex. store for the occasion and is seen arriving at Woking with the 12.19 p.m. Waterloo-Farnborough train on Saturday, 8 July 1950. At the time this was one of 22 Westinghouse fitted former LBSCR / SECR engines borrowed for the event, which included seven members of the B4X class. This would be almost the last regular duty apart, as apart from a few workings around Christmas and New Year 1950 the engines were stored at New Cross and Eastbourne. On paper at least, No. 2052 was one of the last two to be withdrawn in December 1951. (2-30-2)

Opposite top - 'S15' class 4-6-0 No. 30835 is a rare sight at Folkestone Junction on Saturday, 14 June 1958, seen entering the sidings with the 4.25 a.m. special train from Fishguard Harbour. The train is believed to be conveying pilgrims travelling from Ireland en-route to Lourdes, the 'S15' having taken charge at Redhill, leaving there at 12.43 p.m. The arrival time at Folkestone Harbour is not recorded. (6-66-7)

Opposite bottom - The lengthy 9.23 a.m. Willesden Junction - Newhaven Harbour empty stock train approaches Balcombe Tunnel on the down relief line behind a pair of 4-4-0s, 'E1' class No. 31506 and 'Schools' class No.30911 'Dover'. Sunday, 14 April 1957. (6-6-8)

Above - Empty stock from Chatham Dockyard to Rotherhithe Road Carriage Sidings, Bermondsey, is hauled along the Dockyard branch line on Saturday, 4 June 1960, behind two 'C' class 0-6-0s, Nos. 31267 and 31717. Upon arrival at Gillingham, the pair will run around their train and head for London via Strood, tender-first. (3-31-1)

Opposite top - Crosti boilered '9F' class 2-10-0 No. 92028 provides a possibly unique sight on Wednesday, 7 September 1955, leaving Redhill light engine to Brighton for inspection at Brighton Works. The loco has travelled from Wellingborough via the West London line and returned by the same route two days later having been turned on the Preston Park - Hove triangle, not being permitted to enter Brighton loco. yard. (1-19-7)

Opposite bottom - An unwelcome visitor in the shape of ex. LMS 'Jubilee' class 4-6-0 No. 45672 'Anson' is noted passing Purley Oaks en-route to Willesden on Thursday, 2 July 1964. Having arrived at Eastbourne on 19 June 1964 with a train from the LMR, it was used on local duties until failing on 21 June 1964, subsequently being impounded by Brighton Shed. (9-15-1)

Above - 'H' class 0-4-4-T No. 31533 propels inspection saloon No. DS1 near Swifts Green Signalbox (between Headcorn and Pluckley) on an engineers run from Sevenoaks, Saturday 25 March 1961. (3-67-3)

'Battle of Britain' pacifics Nos. 34087 '145 Squadron' (leading) and 34089 '602 Squadron' provide unusual company for a London Transport Bakerloo Line train at Watford High Street whilst turning on the Croxley Junction triangle, Saturday, 12 March 1960. Both locomotives had worked excursions for the Women's International Hockey Final at Wembley. (3-2-4)